CONTINENTS
OF THE WORLD

SOUTH
AMERICA

Simon Scoones

First published in 2005 by Hodder Wayland,
an imprint of Hodder Children's Books

© Hodder Wayland 2005

Commissioning editor: Victoria Brooker
Editor: Kelly Davis
Inside design: Jane Hawkins
Cover design: Hodder Wayland

Series concept and project management by
EASI-Educational Resourcing
(info@easi-er.co.uk)
Statistical research: Anna Bowden

Population Distribution Map
© 2003 UT-Battelle, LLC. All rights reserved.
Data for population distribution maps reproduced under licence from UT-Battelle, LLC.
All rights reserved.

Maps and graphs: Martin Darlison, Encompass Graphics

British Library Cataloguing in Publication Data

Scoones, Simon
  South America. – (Continents of the world)
  1. South America – Juvenile literature
  2. I.Title
  3. 980

ISBN 0 7502 4676 6

Printed and bound in China

Hodder Children's Books
A division of Hodder Headline Limited
338 Euston Road, London NW1 3BH

Picture acknowledgements
The author and publisher would like to thank the following for allowing their
pictures to be reproduced in this publication:
Corbis 12 (Bettmann), 18 (Reuters), 19 (Jhon Jairo Bonilla/Reuters), 24, 40 and
45 (Ricardo Azoury), 39 (Julia Waterlow), 42 (Fulvio Roiter), 44 (Jeremy Horner),
46 (Paulo Whitaker), 47 (Enrique Marcarian), 51(t) (Antoine Serra/In Visu), 51(b)
(David Mercado), 52 (Arianespace); EASI-Images 6, 23 and title page, 31, 36,
and 50 (Roy Maconachie), 3, 8, 9(b), 14(t), 14(b), 16, 21(b), cover main and 26, 27, 30, 34, 35,
57(t) and 57(b) (Simon Scoones); Mary Evans Picture Library 10, 11(t), 11(b);
Panos Pictures 33, 49 and 59 (Jeremy Horner); Edward Parker 4, 9(t), 17, 28, 37,
38, 41, 48, 55, 58; Still Pictures 7 (Gerard and Margi Moss), 13 and 25 (Russell
Gordon), 20 (Kevin Schafer), 21(t) (Mike Kolloffel), 29 and 32 (Mark Edwards),
43 (Janet Jarman), 53 (Ron Giling), cover inset and 54 (Jeremy Woodhouse), 56 (C. Allan Morgan);
Survival 22 (Fiona Watson).

Main cover picture: From 1763 until 1960, Rio de Janeiro was Brazil's capital city.
Because of its beautiful setting, Rio's residents often call it 'The Marvellous City'.

At Iguazú (Iguaçu) Falls, shared by Brazil and
Argentina, there are 259 falls pouring 5,000 cubic
metres (6,500 cubic yards) of water per second.

CONTENTS

SOUTH AMERICA – A LAND OF EXTREMES

South America can boast many record-breaking facts. The continent has some of the world's biggest waterfalls, including the highest. The world's driest desert, Atacama, is found on the western side of the continent. And snaking across the continent's lowlands is the mighty Amazon, a river that carries more water than any other on Earth.

South America rises to extremely high altitudes too. In the west, life for people in Ecuador, Peru and Bolivia is dominated by the Andes, the longest mountain chain on Earth, which stretches for over 8,000 km (5,000 miles). Forced upwards by the collision of vast interlocking pieces of rock that make up the Earth's crust, known as plates, the highest peaks of the Andes rise steeply to nearly 7,000 m (23,000 feet). The world's highest railway winds its way through the Andes in Peru, while La Paz in neighbouring Bolivia is the world's highest capital city.

Deforestation in the Amazon rainforest, Brazil.

In the north, Colombia, Venezuela, Guyana, Suriname and French Guiana lie close to the equator. Much of this region is covered by dense tropical rainforest. Brazil has the biggest expanse of tropical rainforest in the world. Part of this vast natural environment is under threat from farmers, cattle ranchers, loggers, miners and road-builders. Everyone in the world feels the effects of rainforest destruction. Plant species that could become new sources of food or medicine may be lost, and fewer trees are left to soak up the carbon dioxide that contributes to global warming.

Further south, past the plains and cattle ranches of landlocked Paraguay, the republic of Uruguay and northern Argentina, the climate cools until we reach Patagonia, a vast region of ice and snow. This freezing climate is shared by Argentina and Chile in the deep south, a short hop from Antarctica.

Each South American country has its own character. Many enjoy relative wealth, thanks to the continent's plentiful supply of farmland, minerals, timber and energy resources. South America has a population of around 370 million, and many people have moved to cities in search of a better quality of life. Here, industries produce goods for sale across the world. Yet the continent's riches are not equally shared, and it will be a massive challenge for governments to give all young South Americans a chance of a bright future.

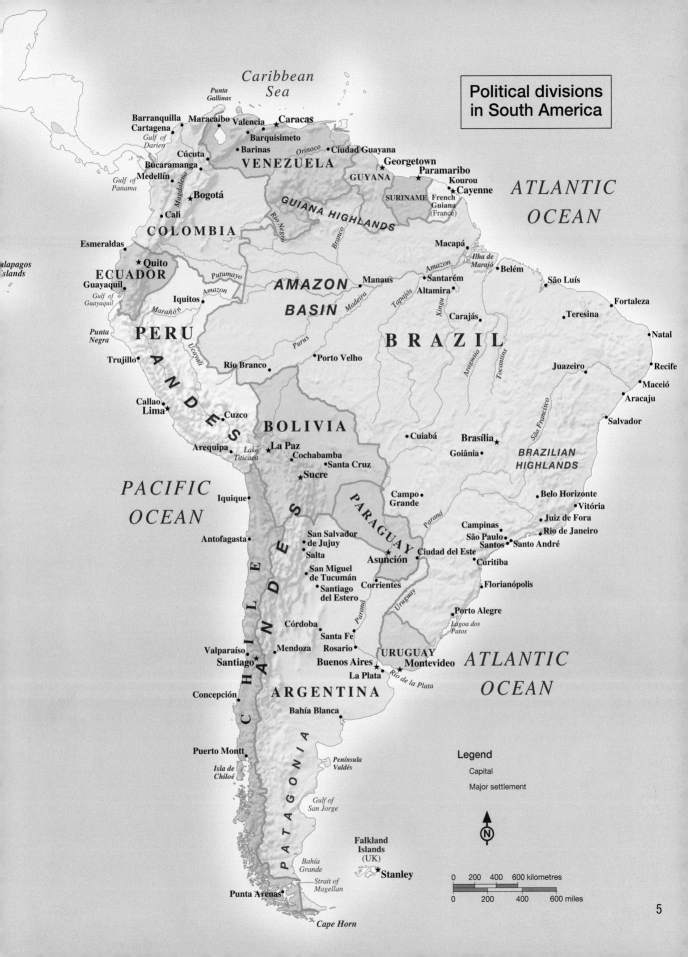

Caribbean Sea

Punta Gallinas

Political divisions in South America

ATLANTIC OCEAN

Barranquilla
Cartagena
Maracaibo • Valencia • Caracas ★
Gulf of Darien
Barquisimeto
Cúcuta • Barinas • Ciudad Guayana
Orinoco
Bucaramanga
VENEZUELA
Georgetown
Paramaribo
Medellín
Gulf of Panama
GUYANA
Kourou
Bogotá ★
SURINAME
Cayenne •
Cali •
GUIANA HIGHLANDS
French Guiana (France)
COLOMBIA
Río Negro
Esmeraldas •
Branco
Macapá •
Galapagos Islands
Quito ★
Putumayo
AMAZON
Ilha de Marajó
ECUADOR
Amazon
Manaus •
Santarém • Belém •
São Luís •
Guayaquil
Altamira •
BASIN
Fortaleza •
Gulf of Guayaquil
Iquitos •
Madeira
Teresina •
Marañón
Amazon
Tapajós
Carajás •
Natal •
Punta Negra
Purus
B R A Z I L
Recife •
PERU
Ucayali
Rio Branco • Porto Velho •
Maceió •
Trujillo •
Juazeiro •
Aracaju
ANDES
Salvador •
Callao
Lima ★ Cuzco •
BOLIVIA
Cuiabá •
Brasília ★
São Francisco
BRAZILIAN
Arequipa • La Paz ★ Cochabamba •
Goiânia •
HIGHLANDS
PACIFIC
Lake Titicaca
Santa Cruz •
Sucre ★
Belo Horizonte •
OCEAN
Iquique •
Campo Grande •
Vitória •
PARAGUAY
Paraná
Campinas • Juiz de Fora •
Rio de Janeiro •
Antofagasta •
San Salvador de Jujuy •
Asunción ★ Ciudad del Este •
São Paulo • Santo André •
Santos •
Salta •
Curitiba •
San Miguel de Tucumán •
Corrientes •
Florianópolis •
Santiago del Estero •
Paraná
Uruguay
Porto Alegre •
Córdoba •
Lagoa dos Patos
Valparaíso •
Santa Fe •
Santiago ★ Mendoza •
Rosario •
URUGUAY
ATLANTIC
Buenos Aires ★
Montevideo ★
Concepción •
La Plata •
Río de la Plata
OCEAN
ARGENTINA
Bahía Blanca •
ANDES
CHILE
Puerto Montt •
Península Valdés
Isla de Chiloé
PATAGONIA
Gulf of San Jorge
Falkland Islands (UK)
Bahía Grande
Stanley ★
Strait of Magellan
Punta Arenas •
Cape Horn

Legend

Capital ★

Major settlement •

N

0 200 400 600 kilometres

0 200 400 600 miles

5

1. THE HISTORY OF SOUTH AMERICA

DURING THE LAST ICE AGE, THE VERY FIRST PEOPLES ARE THOUGHT to have crossed a temporary bridge of solid ice that linked Asia to the western coast of Alaska. Their descendants gradually spread southwards in search of food. About 18,000 years ago, some reached the plains, forests and mountain ranges that we now call Colombia. And groups of American Indians, known as Amerindians, have lived in the tropical rainforests of the Amazon basin for around 15,000 years.

Further south, in Argentina, archaeologists discovered a cave covered in paintings of hands and hunting scenes hidden in the steep rock walls of a canyon, 50 m (160 feet) above the Rio Pinturas. The artists were the Tehuelche people who lived here from 7000 BC and still live in Argentina today. They used the juice of local berries as paint, blown through the carved bone of a nandú, a South American relative of the ostrich. These ancient paintings have remained bright and colourful, thanks to the mixture of fats and urine used by the Tehuelche to preserve them.

For hundreds of years, llamas have been used for farming by the Aymara, Amerindian people who live in Peru and Bolivia.

Around the time of the Tehuelche's cave art, people began to adopt a more settled way of life. By cross-breeding wild plants, they created fields of domesticated potatoes, maize, beans and peppers. They developed sophisticated irrigation techniques to water their fields, and learned how to preserve food by freeze-drying it in the cold mountain air. They also tamed animals like dogs and llamas to help them with their farm work.

●●●●●● ▶ IN FOCUS: Nasca lines

Flying over the stony desert in northern Peru in the 1930s, a scientist called Paul Kosok spotted vast drawings of animals, birds and other patterns etched into the desert. In such a dry climate, rainwater had not washed away the patterns, and they looked much as they had 2,000 years earlier, at the time of the people of Nasca (a small town to the south). An early theory suggested that they could be landing strips for aliens. Although this theory was dismissed long ago, no one is exactly sure why the people drew these images.

Maria Reiche, a German mathematician, devoted her life to studying the Nasca lines. For over fifty years, she charted the lines from the air and from a 15 metre (50 foot) high platform. Maria Reiche believed that the drawings mapped the position of the stars, providing an early form of calendar.

The Nasca lines from the air, depicting a gigantic spider. Researchers think that people started creating these images in about 200 BC and continued for another thousand years.

THE INCA EMPIRE

Farmers moved from Lake Titicaca to settle in the valleys around Cuzco, Peru. Here, around 1100 AD, the great civilization of the Incas began. According to local legend, the first Inca ruler, Manco Capac, rose out of Lake Titicaca. After Manco Capac, a succession of Inca rulers, known as Sapa Inca, controlled Inca territory. Four viceroys looked after Sapa Inca's affairs in the four provinces of the empire. Beneath the viceroys, a governor had authority over ordinary people in each province.

The Incas were skilled architects and road-builders. They built 23,000 km (14,000 miles) of roads, many of which can still be seen today. The Incas were expert farmers too. Near Cuzco, they carved perfect amphitheatres of terraces, and used them to find out what crops grew best at different altitudes. The Incas produced 3,000 types of potato, maize and other crops in these 'open-air laboratories'.

The Colca canyon in southern Peru was a sacred place for the Incas. They believed this was the home of Nevado Ampato, a god who brought them good harvests. To please Nevado

In their great amphitheatres, the Incas could copy soil and moisture conditions at different elevations on the terraces. In this way, they could find out which crops would grow best in different places.

Ampato, the Incas led pilgrimages to the top of Mount Ampato, overlooking the canyon. Here, they would make the ultimate offering – the sacrifice of one of their own people. In 1995, the body of one of the sacrificial victims, named Juanita, was found on the mountain. Thanks to the icy climate, Juanita's body and clothes were perfectly preserved – and can tell us much about how the Incas lived.

Between 1100 and 1500 AD, the Incas conquered other peoples and eventually commanded the biggest empire ever known in the Americas. They introduced the language of Quechua, which is still spoken by people in Bolivia, Colombia, Ecuador and Peru.

A mummy from the ancient Paracas culture, made by people in south-west Peru (1300 BC-200 AD).

●●●●▶ IN FOCUS: The lost city of Machu Picchu

The ancient Inca city of Machu Picchu was discovered in 1911. Built on a ridge above the Urubamba river, at an altitude of 2,350 m (7,710 feet), Machu Picchu had been hidden in the jungle for hundreds of years. Although the forest has been cleared, some mystery still surrounds the ruins.

Most people believe that noble Inca families and their servants lived in Machu Picchu, where they worshipped their sun god. But the fate of the city's residents remains unknown. Today, Machu Picchu is one of Peru's top tourist attractions.

Machu Picchu, Peru.

EUROPEAN INVADERS

At the height of their power, in 1525, the Incas controlled an area bigger than the Roman empire, stretching about 4,000 km (2,500 miles), from northern Ecuador to southern Chile. The Inca empire was home to as many as 12 million people, a third of all South Americans at the time. However by the 1530s, the Inca empire had grown weak and two sons of the former ruler, Huayna (sometimes Wayna) Capac, fought over who should succeed their father. At the same time, explorers from Europe had landed in different parts of the continent, in search of gold and other precious metals. With only 200 men, the Spanish explorer Francisco Pizarro overcame the Inca empire in just two years. A great civilization that had lasted 400 years was over, and much of the continent gradually fell into Spanish hands. Many local people had to give up their land, and were forced to work on plantations, or to mine gold and diamonds. As the Spanish colonies were only permitted to trade with their colonial masters, all these riches were sent to Europe.

Parts of South America were controlled by other European powers. Brazil became a Portuguese colony, and French Guiana is still under French control today. Guyana and Suriname were British colonies. The British set up sugar and tobacco plantations on the banks of the Suriname River around 1650. Two decades later, the

A group of Incas near a stone bridge over a waterfall, as first encountered by Francisco Pizarro and his men in around 1530.

Dutch took over, after doing a deal with the British to swap Suriname with New Amsterdam (present-day New York).

DISEASE AND SLAVERY

The arrival of the Europeans was disastrous for the Amerindians. In the early days, contact between Europeans and Amerindians was quite friendly as the Europeans were fascinated by Amerindian culture. But attitudes changed. The invaders wanted to make the most of their conquered lands, and many Amerindians were murdered or forced to become plantation workers. Other Amerindians died from diseases like measles and smallpox introduced by the Europeans, and many moved deeper into the Amazon rainforest. By the seventeenth century, there were so few Amerindians left on the coast that slaves were shipped over from West Africa to work on the tobacco and sugar plantations.

West African slaves, who have just landed in Suriname in 1806, are handed over to their Dutch master.

Fernando Magellan discovers the Straits of Magellan, Chile, November 1520.

FACT FILE

In the far south, European explorers came across the Tehuelche people. According to Fernando Magellan, the first to encounter them in 1520, the Tehuelche were built like giants. Magellan called them *pata gones* (meaning 'large feet') and Tehuelche territory in southern Argentina and Chile is now called Patagonia.

By the early 1800s, the Spanish had fallen behind both France and Great Britain as a world power. In 1808 the French emperor, Napoleon, invaded Spain. News of Spain's troubles gave hope to those fighting for freedom in South America. Wars of independence broke out, and some parts of the continent changed hands.

HERO OF HEROES

Venezuelan-born Simon Bolívar became the hero of the independence movement. In Peru, the stronghold of the Spanish, Bolívar combined forces with General José de San Martín who had defeated Spanish forces in Argentina. Bolívar drove out the Spanish in Venezuela, Colombia and Ecuador, and won independence for Peruvians in 1821.

The southern part of Peru was renamed Bolivia in honour of General Simon Bolívar (1783-1830), shown here in a painting.

FROM INDEPENDENCE TO DICTATORSHIP

Apart from French Guiana, the rest of South America gained independence during the 1800s. However, in many countries, power was kept in the hands of a few. For instance, in 1973, General Augusto Pinochet Ugarte and his troops organized a coup to remove Salvador Allende, Chile's first freely elected president (who came to power in 1970). In the violence that followed the 1973 coup, Allende was killed and Pinochet began a period of brutal dictatorship that lasted more than fifteen years.

In 1954, Alfredo Stroessner seized power in Paraguay and ruled for nearly thirty-five years. Paraguay became a haven

FACT FILE

In the early 1800s Uruguay was a Spanish colony, before being seized by Great Britain in 1807. Spain took control again, then Argentina, then Portugal, then Brazil. Finally, Uruguay became independent in 1825.

IN FOCUS: Evita

In 1945, a beautiful actress called Eva Perón was adored across Argentina. Best-known as Evita, Eva Perón was President Juan Perón's wife, and she made passionate speeches about the terrible living conditions of the poor. Using her influence on Juan Perón, she forced a change in the law that allowed women to vote for the first time. When Evita died in 1952, the whole country went into mourning.

for Nazis escaping from Europe after the Second World War. Military dictatorships controlled Brazil and Argentina too. From 1976, Argentina's military government began a 'dirty war' to wipe out any opposition to its power. Up to 30,000 people were tortured or secretly killed. But after President Leopoldo Galtieri's failed attempt to take possession of the neighbouring Falkland Islands from the British in 1982, the military government was humiliated. The following year, the generals gave up power and the Argentinian people were allowed to vote freely for their government. Today, people in South America are able to vote freely for their leaders, but older generations have not forgotten the difficult days of dictatorship.

On Thursdays, the 'Mothers of the Disappeared' still gather in Buenos Aires to remember their lost loved ones who were victims of Argentina's 'dirty war'.

2. SOUTH AMERICAN ENVIRONMENTS

Sand dunes in Coro, Venezuela.

During the wet season, between January and March, the Amazon river rises by 20 m (65 feet) to flood an area the size of England (or the state of Iowa).

STRETCHING FROM THE EQUATOR SOUTH TOWARDS THE South Pole, the continent covers a great range of latitudes. The relief of the land varies too, from the high peaks of the Andes to the flat grassland plains and the low-lying Amazon basin. With so many different conditions, the continent has an extraordinary variety of environments. In Venezuela, great grassland plains known as *llanos* cover a third of the country. Along the northern tropical coast, there are coral reefs and vast sand dunes. In the east, highlands give way to the rainforest of the Amazon basin. Meanwhile in the west, snow covers the high peaks of the Andes mountain range.

THE AMAZING AMAZON

Lying near the equator, plants and trees grow all year round in the Amazon basin, making it the world's biggest area of tropical rainforest. Many parts of the rainforest remain untouched by human activities, and scientists believe that it may contain up to 20,000 undiscovered plant species.

Some areas of the Amazon receive over 6,000 mm (236 inches) of rainfall in a year, but there is plenty of sunshine too. These year-round hot, wet conditions speed up the rate at which nutrients are released from the dead plants rotting on the forest

floor. Tree roots quickly absorb the nutrients through their roots to reuse them. Thanks to this rapid cycle of growth and decay, trees in the Amazon can climb to amazing heights even though the soils are of poor quality. This incredible environment also boasts the greatest variety of plant species to be found anywhere on Earth.

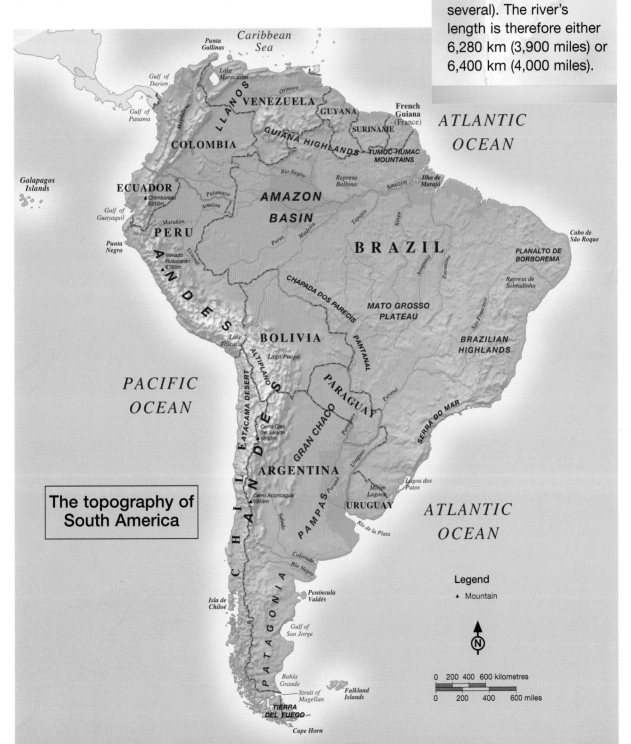

The topography of South America

Legend

▲ Mountain

N

| 0 | 200 | 400 | 600 kilometres |
| 0 | 200 | 400 | 600 miles |

RAINFORESTS OF THE SEA

The tropical waters along the continent's Caribbean coast are home to millions of polyps (tiny aquatic animals) that join to form vast coral reefs. These are sometimes called 'the rainforests of the sea' because of the thousands of sea creatures that live on them. Coral reefs are very delicate. Some corals will die just from someone touching them. Changes in water temperature and murky water can also kill coral, turning an underwater paradise into a dull wasteland. Along Colombia's coast, fishermen have added to the problem by over-fishing the waters around the coral reefs. To prevent further damage, the Tayrona National Park extends for 185 sq km (115 sq miles) into the sea. Rangers keep watch, and scientists regularly monitor the health of the reefs.

FACT FILE

Before the uplift of the Andes mountains, the River Amazon emptied into the Pacific Ocean rather than flowing eastwards to the Atlantic Ocean as it does today.

MIGHTY MOUNTAINS

Many of the continent's environments are influenced by the Andes. This immense mountain range began forming 60 million years ago when the Nasca plate beneath the Pacific Ocean was forced beneath the South America plate, pushing the land upwards. Towering to a height of 6,960 m (22,800 feet), Mount Aconcagua in Argentina is the highest mountain outside Asia. Because the Earth's plates continue to

El Misti, a beautiful snow-capped mountain, towers over the city of Arequipa in Peru.

The Tren de la Sierra ('Mountain Train') climbs from Peru's capital, Lima, at sea level, up into the Andes. In the Andes the train reaches an altitude of 4,829 m (15,800 feet), which is half the height of Mount Everest. At this altitude, the air has 40 per cent less oxygen than at sea level. This is partly why it took so long to build the railway. Starting in 1869, and facing great hardship and danger, the railway workers carved 66 tunnels through the mountains and built 59 bridges over land prone to floods and landslides. Around two thousand workers died before the railway was finally completed in 1908.

collide, parts of the Andes range are still growing. Movements of the plates force molten rock onto the surface, making some mountains into active volcanoes.

FORESTS IN THE MIST

The warmth of the tropics enables trees to grow high on mountain slopes, at altitudes of up to 3,000 m (10,000 feet). Often cloaked in mist, these 'cloud forests' receive 6,000 mm (236 inches) of rain a year. Cloud forests are magical places.

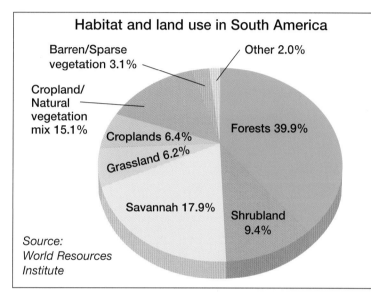

Habitat and land use in South America

Barren/Sparse vegetation 3.1%
Other 2.0%
Cropland/Natural vegetation mix 15.1%
Croplands 6.4%
Grassland 6.2%
Forests 39.9%
Savannah 17.9%
Shrubland 9.4%

Source: World Resources Institute

Almost every hillside has its own special plants and animals. Tree trunks are gnarled and stunted by the rain, sun and mountain winds, and the forest is rich with mosses and ferns. Rotting leaves collect on tree branches. As they break down, they make a kind of soil that provides food for epiphytes. These epiphytes create a hanging garden in the trees, attracting beautiful hummingbirds in need of nectar, and thousands of insects.

Epiphytes in a cloud forest on Mount Cotopaxi, Ecuador. Mount Cotopaxi lies almost on the equator. Yet, at 5,897 m (19,300 feet) high, it is always covered with snow. Cotopaxi is also the highest active volcano in the world.

FACT FILE

The Amazon is the world's largest river. It discharges an average of 200,000 cubic metres (7,100,000 cubic feet) of water per second.

SAILING UP THE RIVER

Although the River Amazon begins from water gushing down the steep slopes of the Andes, the rest of the river's journey to the sea is spent winding across the low-lying Amazon basin. Large boats can sail 1,600 km (1,000 miles) up the river to the Brazilian city of Manaus because Manaus is only 30 m (100 feet) higher than the river's mouth.

QUAKES AND TSUNAMIS

In South America there are many hazards to human life. There are even dangers beneath the ground people walk on. Pressure can build up between the plates of the Earth's crust as they grind together beneath the continent. When this pressure is released, shock waves radiate outwards in the form of an earthquake.

A major earthquake, registering 8.1 on the Richter scale, struck Arequipa, Peru's second-biggest city, in June 2001. The city shook for more than a minute, and the tremors were felt hundreds of kilometres away. About a hundred people died and thousands more were injured. The earthquake also damaged three-quarters of the city's buildings, including the historic cathedral. Along the coast, towns and villages were hit by a tsunami, whipped up by the earthquake as the ocean water surged 800 m (2,600 feet) inland.

A resident of Arequipa steps over the debris left after the earthquake struck in 2001.

EL NIÑO

There are also dangers in the weather. In the nineteenth century, Peruvian fishermen noticed that every five years or so their Pacific fishing waters were unusually warm. This change in the climate was named El Niño or 'the Christ child', as it normally happened around Christmas time. Scientists are still puzzled by El Niño, but they think it starts when there is a change in the interaction between the ocean waters and the atmosphere. In an El Niño year, the trade winds are not strong enough to pull the warm waters away from the South American coast. Instead, warm air and ocean currents, flowing from west to east, stop the cooler water of the Humboldt ocean current from reaching the surface.

El Niño is bad news for fishermen. The water is too warm for the anchovies and sardines that they normally catch. The warmer ocean also triggers torrential rains that flood coastal towns and villages in southern Peru. During the February 2003 El Niño, a deluge of rainwater destroyed fields of crops and 6,000 homes, and killed 18 people. The stagnant pools of water left behind by the floods and the warmer temperatures also created a breeding ground for mosquitoes, carrying diseases like malaria. Nevertheless, this El Niño was weaker than the previous one. In 1997-98, the strongest El Niño on record killed more than 200 people in floods and landslides, and caused damage estimated at over US$3.5 billion dollars.

Rescue teams sift through rock and mud which buried homes in the village of Mistrato, about 250 km (155 miles) north-west of Bogotá, Colombia, after torrential rains caused a mudslide in 2003.

A LOST WORLD

In an area only accessible by air or by river in South-East Venezuela, 40 flat-topped mountains rise out of the dense rainforest. Amerindians believed that these 'table top mountains', or *tepuis*, were the seats of the gods. Made from hard-wearing sandstone, the *tepuis*, part of the Guiana Highlands, are up to 400 million years old. At this time, South America, along with other continents, was part of one gigantic landmass called Gondwanaland. Plunging 979 m (3,212 feet) down the vertical walls of a *tepuis* is a waterfall named after Jimmy Angel, an American pilot who first spotted it from the air in 1935. Angel Falls is the world's highest waterfall, 15 times higher than Niagara. Much of this beautiful wilderness is now protected as part of Canaima National Park. Spreading over 3 million hectares (7 million acres), Canaima is the third-largest national park in the world.

Angel Falls, Venezuela.

FACT FILE

There are some parts of the Atacama desert where there is no record of rain ever having fallen.

HIGH AND DRY

The Humboldt ocean current, which brings cold air northwards, stops rain clouds from developing over the Atacama desert. This sometimes means that it does not rain for years. At the same time, the chilly air cools the desert's temperatures to a maximum of 24°C (75°F).

Part of the Atacama desert rises to high altitudes. The *altiplano*, or high plain, is one of the most hostile environments on Earth. As the air is too thin to keep its heat, temperatures can drop to -25°C (-13°F) at night. On the *altiplano*, salt lakes form as meltwater and dissolved salts wash off the mountains. During the day, water evaporates, leaving behind the salty deposits. In the winter, some salt lakes freeze over.

THE WORLD'S END

Beyond the grasslands of Argentina and Paraguay, we reach an icy wilderness. Here in Patagonia, the Great Southern Icefield covers 11,300 sq km (7,000 sq miles), the biggest expanse of ice outside the Poles. In Patagonia, ferocious storms – with hurricane-force winds and hailstones the size of golfballs – are a risk, even in the summer. Glaciers stick out like fingers from the edge of the icefield, acting like rivers of ice. As more ice is formed, the glaciers move very slowly, scouring and stripping the mountains in their path. But in recent years, some glaciers have actually started shrinking as global climate change has brought warmer temperatures to Patagonia.

The Salar de Uyuni on Bolivia's *altiplano*, is the highest and largest salt lake in the world. Here, people mine the salt at 3,653 m (12,000 feet) above sea level. This spectacular lake also attracts many tourists.

Perito Moreno glacier, Patagonia. As parts of the glacier melt, huge chunks of this 50 m (160 foot) high wall of ice break off and crash into the lake.

3. THE PEOPLE OF SOUTH AMERICA

WHEN EUROPEANS FIRST CAME TO SOUTH AMERICA IN THE 1500s, around two million Amerindians were living in the Amazon rainforest.

In 2003, the remaining 300 Awá people who live in Brazil's Amazon rainforest finally won rights to their lands after a 20-year struggle with the Brazilian government.

Each group developed its own way of life and set of beliefs, and there are still 170 different languages spoken in the Amazon basin. But there are now fewer than a million Amerindians left in the rainforest, and many groups face extinction.

Elsewhere, other Amerindian groups have disappeared. In Tierra del Fuego, on the southernmost tip of the continent, Amerindians used to hunt game on the barren plains. But in 1877, an English trader called Henry Reynard introduced sheep to the area. Tensions grew because the Amerindians found it easier to hunt the farmers' sheep rather than wild game. Many Amerindians were killed in revenge, while others died from diseases which had been brought over by the Europeans. Around 40 per cent of the Nukak, an Amerindian group in the Colombian Amazon, have died from respiratory diseases like flu and tuberculosis (TB).

A RIGHT TO LAND

Without laws to guarantee Amerindian land rights, loggers, ranchers and new settlers are still taking over territory that has been home to Amerindian groups for generations. However, the Nukak have been more fortunate. They have been given land rights to their territory in Colombia, protecting their livelihood for the future.

The Aymara and Pacha Mama

Peru, Bolivia and Ecuador are home to the biggest populations of Amerindian groups, like the Aymara. Although they were previously dominated by the Incas and then the Spanish, the Aymara have retained their own culture and language and are now self-governed. They still live on the high, barren plains of the *altiplano* on the shores of Lake Titicaca in Peru and Bolivia.

Like most Amerindians, the Aymara believe that they belong to the land and what they take from the environment should be repaid in some way. According to the Aymara, Pacha Mama ('Mother Earth') helps crops and animals grow. At certain times, they thank Pacha Mama with offerings of coca leaves and animal fat, and by sprinkling a type of alcohol on the ground.

An Aymara woman in Bolivia weaves brightly coloured cloth. With a population of about 14 million in Peru, Bolivia and Ecuador, the Aymara are the largest Amerindian group in South America. The Aymara are descendants of people who were once ruled by the Incas.

FACT FILE

South of the Amazon basin, 17 Ayoreo Amerindians emerged from the forests of Paraguay and made contact with the outside world for the first time in March 2004. These people had been forced out of the forest, after their precious water holes and much of their land had been taken over illegally by ranchers and other farmers.

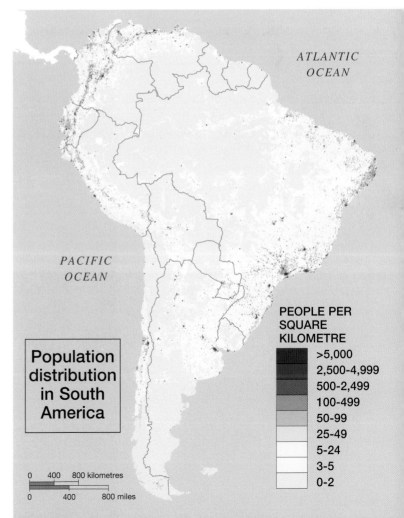

ATLANTIC OCEAN

PACIFIC OCEAN

Population distribution in South America

PEOPLE PER SQUARE KILOMETRE

- >5,000
- 2,500-4,999
- 500-2,499
- 100-499
- 50-99
- 25-49
- 5-24
- 3-5
- 0-2

0   400   800 kilometres

0   400   800 miles

MIXED BACKGROUNDS

Relationships between Spanish and Amerindian people were widespread in colonial times, and many South Americans today are *mestizo* (of mixed Amerindian and Spanish background). Others are descendants of West African slaves.

People in Suriname have an extraordinary variety of backgrounds. Some can trace their roots back to West Africa and Indonesia, as descendants of slaves brought over by the British or Dutch. Hindustanis make up a third of Suriname's population. They first came from northern India in the late 1800s. By this time slavery had been abolished, and Hindustanis came to work on Suriname's plantations in return for food, clothes and shelter. After centuries of intermarriage, another third of Suriname's people are Creole (a mixture of black and white).

FACT FILE

The family of Alberto Fujimori, Peru's president from 1990 to 2000, originally came from Japan. Thousands of Brazilians also have Japanese heritage.

A Guaraní man and child hold crosses as part of a religious ceremony in Paraguay. Like their language, Paraguayans have adapted customs introduced to them by missionaries since the 1600s.

●●●► IN FOCUS:
Spanish/Guarani

Unlike other South Americans, Paraguayans kept their local language, Guaraní, during colonial times. Visiting missionaries from Europe grew fond of the sound of Guaraní, and intermarriage between local people and the Spanish was widespread. Today, most Paraguayans can speak both Spanish and Guaraní.

Argentina's population is almost entirely of European origin. About three million Italians moved to Argentina in the late nineteenth and early twentieth centuries, along with people from other parts of Europe. Smaller groups of immigrants have settled here too. In the mountainous province of Chubut, Welsh was the second language until the 1990s.

The gauchos are the cowboys of Argentina, admired for their courage, self-reliance and love of the land. With their silver spurs, horses and packs of dogs, the gauchos still herd their livestock on *estancias* (ranches) scattered across Argentina's grassland plains.

Many of Argentina's gauchos still wear black Spanish hats and Amerindian shawls, representing their *mestizo* (mixed) background.

ISLAND LIFE

About 500 km (300 miles) off the coast of Argentina, people on the Falkland Islands (or Las Malvinas, as they are known in Argentina) speak English, and make a living from fishing, sheep farming and oil exploration. Despite Argentina's attempt to seize control of the islands in the 1982 Falklands War, they have remained in British hands since 1833. In many ways, Falkland Islanders have more in common with Britain than with the rest of South America. Today, nearly half the residents of the islands are British troops, protecting the islands.

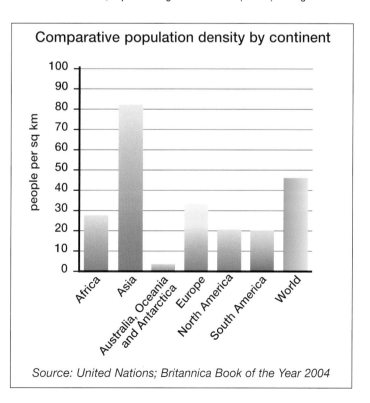

Comparative population density by continent

people per sq km

Source: United Nations; Britannica Book of the Year 2004

From 1763 until 1960, Rio de Janeiro was Brazil's capital city. Because of its beautiful setting, Rio's residents often call it 'The Marvellous City'.

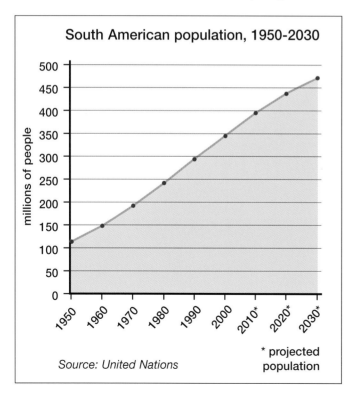

South American population, 1950-2030

Source: United Nations

* projected population

In 1900, there were around forty million people in South America and the population growth rate was high. Many men wanted large families as a sign of status, and farming families needed children to work on the land. At the same time, large numbers of people moved from Europe to make a new start in South America. Although birth rates have since slowed down, the total population of the continent is today nearly ten times greater than it was a hundred years ago. The majority of people now live in towns and cities, much like industrialized countries. Many have left a life of poverty in the countryside and moved to cities in search of a better standard of living. Population growth within the cities themselves adds to the urban sprawl. Nevertheless, many South Americans find it difficult to make a living, and poverty puts great stress on families.

The growth of cities has led to environmental problems that affect all South Americans. In Santiago, Chile, the five million residents have to cope with one of the highest levels of air pollution in the world. Smoke, gases and particles become trapped like a blanket over the city; and over a million cars spew out pollutants, adding to the problem. Many people suffer from illnesses caused by the pollution, and the city authorities are now taking action to clean up the city. They have introduced buses that run on cleaner fuels, and on days when pollution levels are particularly high the city authorities order factories to close.

FACT FILE

More than 80 per cent of Brazilians and nearly 90 per cent of Argentinians live in towns and cities, and there are 15 cities with more than a million residents in Brazil. Over 15 million people live in the Brazilian city of São Paolo.

●●●●●●▶ IN FOCUS: A boost for the *favelas*

In Rio de Janeiro, a fifth of the residents live in poor neighbourhoods, or *favelas*, scattered around the city on waste ground or on one of Rio's many steep ravines. Over the last decade, the city authorities have invested in a programme called the 'Favela Bairio' to create a better quality of life for these residents. In one neighbourhood, Villa Canoas, a new sewage system and waste collection service has reduced the risk of disease, particularly among children. Educational facilities have improved too, with a new community school and a training centre for adults.

Building on the skills and strong community spirit among Villa Canoas residents, the programme has helped new businesses flourish, like this locally run company that makes apple strudel.

Many families move to towns and cities so that their children can go to better schools. Yet poverty often forces the children to earn money for the family instead. Across South America, school drop-out rates are so high that the average time spent at school (five years) can be lower than it is in poorer parts of Africa. Primary education is free in Brazil, yet nearly a fifth of Brazilians cannot read or write. With fewer educated people, it becomes more difficult to find well-qualified teachers to work in schools, and the gap between rich people qualified for well-paid jobs and others without an education continues to grow.

LIFE ON THE STREET

Many children living on the streets of cities like Rio de Janeiro, in Brazil, have never been to school. For some, the streets are a workplace where they earn money to support the rest of the family. For others, the streets are their home, day and night. Some have run away from home because of a family breakdown, or because they have suffered violence and abuse. Street children have to learn to fend for themselves, as their lives can be difficult and dangerous. But, like any children, street children have rights, and they need help to find safe, legal ways of looking after themselves. An organization called Cruzada do Menor ('Children's Crusade') has set up a centre where street children can learn how to read

Some of the homeless children who live on the street in Brazil, looking for food or things to sell.

and write and gain other skills that will improve their chances of getting decent jobs in the city.

HEALTH MATTERS

Although other continents (such as Africa) have more people living with HIV/AIDS, the problem is growing in South America. Doctors think there may be two thousand street children who are HIV-positive in Rio alone. Yet Brazil has become an example to the world in its fight against HIV/AIDS. Thanks to a widespread education programme, Brazilians are more likely to know how to avoid infection. Most Brazilians are Catholic, but even though traditional teachings of the Catholic Church are against using contraceptives, condoms are widely used in Brazil. At the same time, drugs used to suppress the symptoms of HIV/AIDS are virtually free. These drugs are made locally by Brazilian companies and are cheaper than the equivalent drugs sold on the international market.

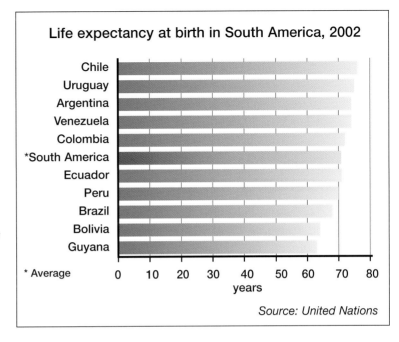

Life expectancy at birth in South America, 2002

Chile
Uruguay
Argentina
Venezuela
Colombia
*South America
Ecuador
Peru
Brazil
Bolivia
Guyana

* Average   0   10   20   30   40   50   60   70   80
years

Source: United Nations

South American teenagers being educated about the dangers of sexually transmitted diseases and HIV and AIDS.

FACT FILE

Adults living with HIV/AIDS in Brazil make up 0.7 per cent of the population, compared to 20.1 per cent in South Africa.

4. SOUTH AMERICAN CULTURE AND RELIGION

TODAY, OVER 80 PER CENT OF SOUTH AMERICANS ARE PRACTISING CATHOLICS. During colonial times, missionaries from Spain and Portugal came to convert Amerindians to Christianity. They travelled far and wide, sometimes learning Amerindian languages in order to explain their faith more easily. Yet, despite the missionaries' efforts, many Amerindian groups have kept their own ancient beliefs. For instance, in Chile, the Mapuche people believe that bad luck, disease and death come from evil magic. Healers, called *machi*, hold special ceremonies to guard against these evils.

Catholic São Francisco church,
Salvador da Bahia, Brazil.

MIXING RELIGIONS

In some parts of the continent, Catholicism has been mixed with other beliefs to form a new religion. In Bahia state, Brazil, Candomblé combines Catholicism with traditional Amerindian customs as well as African beliefs brought over by slaves. A Candomblé ceremony is led by a priest or priestess and may last for several hours. The people call on their gods to possess them by performing dances and songs to the beat of an African drum. The dancers work themselves into a trance, then change into fine costumes and have their bodies painted with intricate patterns. Each dancer then performs a special dance to please one of the gods.

SEPARATE RELIGIONS

Other peoples have brought their own blend of religion to the continent. In 1927, Mennonites came from Canada to settle in Paraguay. Paraguayans welcomed people from elsewhere as many men had been killed in wars, and most of the thorny forests and barren plains of the Chaco in western Paraguay were uninhabited and unused. Originally from Germany, the Mennonites were strict Protestants. They also had a reputation for being skilled farmers and hard workers. In return for their religious freedom and the right to speak German, the Mennonites agreed to occupy the sweltering Chaco plains. Today, there are 28,000 Mennonites in Paraguay, and they run most of the country's dairy farms.

Religions in South America

Other 7.2%
Includes Hinduism (0.1%)
Judaism (0.2%)
Islam (0.3%)
non-religious (0.3%)

Christianity 92.8%

Source: Britannica Book of the Year 2004

●●●●●●● ▶ IN FOCUS: The Day of the Dead

For the Aymara in Peru, 2 November is a very important day. They believe this is the time when the spirits of the dead visit the living. Aymara families prepare breads in different shapes and decorate tombs with sweets, flowers, onions and sugarcane.

The Aymara believe that these gifts will help the spirits of their dead relatives find their way into new bodies and be reincarnated (reborn).

Aymara Day of the Dead celebration in Bolivia.

People in every corner of Brazil celebrate 'Carnivale' and each carnival has its own rhythms, dances and styles.

LET'S RUMBA!

Rumba means 'party' to most South American people – across the continent, parties are big, loud and a lot of fun. In Brazil, the biggest party of them all happens each year just before Lent. 'Carnivale' takes place on the streets of every Brazilian city. For five days and nights, the streets are filled with people in colourful costumes, dancing to the samba beat.

In many poor neighbourhoods, young people practise for months at samba schools in order to be the best samba troupe. But in Rio de Janeiro, many young people dance to funk rather than samba these days. Originating in Brazil, funk mixes rap, techno beats and thudding bass lines.

Meanwhile, at Colombian parties, hips sway to the rhythm of cumbia, which has both local and African influences. The shuffling footwork of cumbia dancing may hark back to the time when African slaves tried to dance with chains around their ankles. Modern cumbia adds hip-hop to the mix, giving it a new lease of life.

LET'S ROCK!

Many young Brazilians and Argentinians are huge rock fans too. In January, Rio de Janeiro stages the 'Rock in Rio' festival, one of the biggest rock concerts in the world, where people flock to see both local and international musicians. In 1985, the first 'Rock in Rio' festival, following many years of military rule in Brazil, was seen as a celebration of freedom.

FOOTBALL CRAZY

South Americans are passionate about soccer. In Brazil, many people take the day off work if the national team is playing. If they score, fireworks light up the sky in many Brazilian cities. The atmosphere is more like a big party – so long as they win! But when the Colombian team lost to the USA and crashed out of the 1994 World Cup, the picture was very different. Colombian defender Andres Escobar had scored an own-goal and was blamed for the defeat. Ten days later, he was murdered in his hometown, Medellín. Escobar's death remains a mystery, but many believe that one of the drug cartels was responsible. They lost millions of dollars on bets because of Colombia's early exit from the competition.

Colombian soccer fans cheer on their team during the Copa América, the oldest national soccer tournament in the world. Since 1916, there have been 41 tournaments. Soccer teams representing countries across the Americas battle it out for the prized trophy. The greatest victors are Argentina and Uruguay – they have won the tournament 14 times each!

STORIES OF MAGICAL REALISM

Some South American authors are famous for their colourful, dream-like stories. This type of writing is known as magical realism. The Nobel prize-winning author Gabriel García Márquez has been influenced by the way in which his grandmother used to tell him stories. Márquez's first book about his own childhood in Aracataca, northern Colombia, called *To live to tell it*, became a best-selling book in the Spanish-speaking world. Another popular magical realist writer is Isabel Allende. She grew up in Chile, and her uncle, Salvador Allende, was president until he was murdered in 1973. Her books have been translated into nearly thirty different languages.

WHAT'S COOKING?

A favourite dish in the coastal communities of Peru and Ecuador is ceviche, made from raw white fish marinated in lemon juice, onions and hot peppers. Traditionally, ceviche was served with corn-on-the-cob, but today many Ecuadorians prefer theirs with a bowl of popcorn.

A plate of ceviche, served with roasted corn kernels and popcorn.

Food is bought and traded at local markets. At Saquisili market in Ecuador, farmers come down from the mountain slopes to trade vegetables for bananas, pigs, cloth or even a few llamas! Market days are also a chance to meet friends and catch up with local gossip.

South Americans are keen meat-eaters too. Argentinians and Uruguayans are proud of their succulent beef steaks, often cooked slowly over an open fire. In the highlands of Peru, people still eat roast

Colourful rugs and wall hangings on sale at a market in Otoválo, Ecuador.

guinea pig, a delicacy since Inca times. Food in Brazil is steeped in history as well, as it draws on the different backgrounds of the country's people. In Bahia state, acarajés are one of the tastiest items on the menu. These spicy snacks use ingredients like palm oil, prawns and peppers, celebrating the people's West African ancestry.

A Cup of Tea

Many South Americans enjoy maté, a kind of tea made from a wild plant. The Guaraní people in Paraguay have been drinking maté for thousands of years. In the past, they believed that maté held magic powers. People still take a break with a cup of maté in modern-day Paraguay. They drink it through a silver straw, from a small, polished gourd, passing it round to share with family or friends.

5. NATURAL RESOURCES IN SOUTH AMERICA

MOST SOUTH AMERICAN COUNTRIES HAVE PLENTIFUL SUPPLIES OF minerals and precious metals. Chile is the world's leading producer of copper, and the country has rich reserves of other resources such as lithium, nitrates and iron ore. Chuquicamata, in northern Chile, about 250 km (155 miles) from Antofagasta, is the largest copper mine in the world. However, mining and smelting copper releases large amounts of pollution into the air and water, which threatens the health of many Chileans. Chuquicamata was once shut down for a whole month because of the extent of the pollution produced by the mine.

A miner in Potosi, Bolivia, mining silver in Cerro Rico ('Rich Mountain').

FACT FILE

Between 1545 and 1660, the Spanish took around 16 million kg (16,000 tons) of Bolivia's silver back to Spain.

NEW DISCOVERIES

Bolivia is also rich in natural resources. In 1544, an Amerindian called Diego Huallpa discovered an enormous supply of silver on the *altiplano*, 4,000 m (13,000 feet) above sea-level. For the next 200 years, the Spanish rulers of Bolivia took most of these riches back to Spain. Tin became another source of wealth for Bolivia. However in the 1980s, the electronics industry, which bought tin, was depressed, so less tin was needed. In 1985 world tin prices collapsed, many tin mines closed down and thousands of Bolivians lost their jobs.

RUMOURS OF RICHES

Argentina means 'the Land of Silver', although this country's rich farmland is a much more important resource than its precious metals. The name came from the first Spanish explorers to reach the country in the early 1500s. When they were shipwrecked at the mouth of the Rio de la Plata ('Silver River'), they were greeted by Amerindians who presented them with silver objects. By 1524, a rumour reached Spain that Argentina had a mountain rich in silver, and many more Spaniards sailed over to find their fortune. But they were disappointed to discover that this was just a local legend.

Other valuable resources lie beneath the Amazon rainforest. At Carajás, the world's largest source of iron ore was discovered when a plane flew over the Brazilian Amazon. The pilot saw a giant red gap in the surrounding green carpet of forest. Since then, trains up to 2 km (1 mile) long have transported the ore out of Carajás, and the vast Tucuruí dam has been built to power its iron-smelting furnaces. The artificial lake behind the dam is bigger than some European countries.

A lead mine in the Andes, near La Oroya, central Peru.

FACT FILE

Gold was the first metal to be used by people in South America – possibly as long ago as 2000 BC in Peru. Today, more than a million miners, known as *garimpeiros*, still come to the Amazon basin in search of gold.

An oil pipeline in the rainforest of Ecuador, near Lago Agrio.

BLACK GOLD

Energy resources, like natural gas and oil, are also very important in South America. Venezuela's oil fields around Lake Maracaibo account for most of the country's export earnings, and Venezuela provides 13 per cent of the USA's oil imports. Ecuador relies on oil for more than a third of its export earnings, after rich deposits were discovered beneath the Amazon rainforest in 1967. The oil is pumped across the Andes, through the Trans-Andean pipeline, to the port of Esmeraldas in the west.

POWER FROM THE AMAZON

The Amazon region is the source of another type of energy – derived from fast-flowing water – hydro-electric power (HEP). Unlike burning oil or coal, HEP does not release harmful gases into the atmosphere. And, so long as there is running water, this type of power will not run out. People build dams to trap the water's energy. Brazil already has 600 large dams, but they have been criticized by environmental groups. When a river is dammed, the flooding behind the dam can destroy houses and farmland, and the still water creates a new breeding ground for mosquitoes. Many people are forced to leave their homes, and very few of them receive compensation.

On the Paraguay–Brazil border, the vast Itaipu dam is currently the world's biggest HEP project. A joint venture between Paraguay and Brazil, the dam harnesses the power of the River Paraná and generates enough energy for nearly all of Paraguay's electricity.

The Itaipu dam is 8 km (5 miles) long and has created a lake or reservoir that covers 1,400 sq km (870 sq miles).

●●●●●▶ IN FOCUS: Selling off Bolivia's assets

Since 1993, with crushing debts and few other ways of making money, the Bolivian government has been selling off the country's natural resources to overseas companies. Yet many Bolivians are very reluctant to give up their country's resources. In Cochabamba, angry residents clashed with police after the government sold the city's water system to foreign owners in 1999. Water bills more than doubled, and people reacted by organizing protest marches and a four-day strike. The government later cancelled the contract. In 2003, protests broke out across Bolivia over plans to pump the country's natural gas to Mexico and the USA. Many people believed that the gas revenues would only line the pockets of a few, mostly foreign investors, while most Bolivians would not benefit at all. These protests forced the President of Bolivia, Gonzalo Sanchez de Lozada, to resign in 2003.

Amerindians gather at Altamira, Brazil, in 1989 to voice their opposition to the proposed dam.

As South America's fastest-growing consumer of energy, Chile has also been investing in HEP. Chileans have been building dams to trap the wild meltwater rivers that run off the slopes of the Andes. But, like the Brazilians who live along the dammed tributaries of the Amazon, life for the people who live along these rivers is changing irreversibly. Meanwhile, some Amerindians in Brazil have been joining forces with environmentalists and human rights activists to fight back against the building of dams.

In February 1989, the Kayapó people gathered at Altamira in the Brazilian Amazon to protest against a massive dam-building project along the Xingu river. Their campaign won worldwide support and the project was abandoned. Had it been built, the dam would have flooded many of the Kayapó's sacred lands.

THE RUBBER INDUSTRY

Rubber used to be an important resource from the Amazon rainforest. When a cut is made in the trunk of a rubber tree, a sticky liquid called latex oozes out. Boosted by the invention of the rubber tyre and the development of steamboats for transport up the river, the rubber industry boomed in the 1800s when nearly all the rubber used worldwide came from the Amazon region. The British then took seeds to South-East Asia to plant vast numbers of rubber trees, and the Amazon's rubber industry collapsed. Nevertheless, by working together in co-operatives, some people still make a living from rubber-tapping.

THE TIMBER TRADE

Timber is another important resource. Thanks to Chile's fertile soil, pine trees grow faster here than in other countries. In tropical areas, hardwoods, such as mahogany, sell for a high price on the world market.

Trade in tropical hardwoods is nothing new. Around five hundred years ago, Amerindians in the Amazon rainforest would trade with Europeans, exchanging mahogany for axes, mirrors and coloured beads. But the timber trade has since spiralled out of control. To meet the high demand for tropical hardwoods in rich countries, loggers destroy large areas of rainforest in search of this precious timber. New networks of roads carve through the rainforest to reach the timber more easily. And, by creating new openings into the forest, these roads encourage more settlers to try their luck in the Amazon, destroying yet more forest.

The Atlantic forest along Brazil's coastline has nearly all gone as people have cleared the land to build houses, grow crops or use the trees as timber.

6. THE SOUTH AMERICAN ECONOMY

A HUNDRED YEARS AGO, ARGENTINA'S PLAINS WERE OPENED UP for cattle ranching on a massive scale. Argentina became by far the richest country in South America. Thousands of poorer Europeans flocked there in search of work on the ranches. During the First and Second World Wars, Argentina and neighbouring Uruguay exported tinned beef in vast quantities to feed hungry people in war-torn Europe. Virtually any crop can be grown in Argentina, thanks to its varied climate which stretches from the tropics to the Antarctic. It is now the world's fifth-biggest exporter of farm products.

GM CONFLICT

Ranch hands rounding up cattle in Argentina.

One of Argentina's most important crops is soya beans. Many Argentinian farmers use genetically modified (GM) soya seeds that can be grown all year round. Until September 2003,

GM crops were banned across Brazil because of concerns that GM pollen or seeds might escape and contaminate non-GM varieties. Some Brazilian farmers also fear that GM crops may increase their dependence on the multinational companies that make and sell the seeds. But GM seeds have already been smuggled into Brazil, contaminating other fields, and angering many Brazilians.

FACT FILE

Around 50 per cent of Argentina's cropland is used to grow GM soya beans. Argentina grows more GM crops than any other country except the United States.

●●●●●●▶ IN FOCUS: Dollar bananas

Ecuador is the world's largest exporter of bananas. About a quarter of the bananas eaten in the USA and a fifth of bananas eaten in Europe come from Ecuador. Ecuadorian bananas are sometimes called 'dollar bananas' because they are very cheap. One reason for their low price is that labourers (some of them children) work long hours for very low wages on Ecuador's vast plantations.

Many plantations are owned by multinational companies. To produce as many bananas as possible, some of these companies use a lot of chemicals to kill insect pests and make the bananas grow faster. But these chemicals can pollute the environment, and may cause health problems.

Plantation workers are at particular risk. Some have no protective clothing, even though these chemicals can cause cancer and infertility. Fortunately, some companies (both big corporations and small farming co-operatives linked to Fair Trade schemes) are now starting to grow bananas in ways that are less harmful to the environment, using fewer chemicals and recycling waste.

Labelling bananas in Ecuador for sale abroad.

Most of Colombia's coffee is grown on small, family-run farms, and the farmers rely on people, rather than machines, to pick the coffee beans.

CHANGING WORLD PRICES

As well as farm products, other raw materials, known as primary products, are important to South American economies. Oil dominates the economies of Venezuela, Ecuador and Colombia, and Chile depends on selling copper for half its wealth.

When prices fall on the world market, the countries that rely on selling these primary products can find themselves in trouble. When copper prices plummeted in the late 1990s, unemployment and debt rose in Chile. Since then, rising copper prices have improved the fortunes of some Chileans. Colombia's 560,000 coffee farmers have had a tougher time. With more countries producing coffee worldwide, prices have plunged to an all-time low. Many coffee farmers in Colombia have decided to give up altogether. Others are joining together to grow Fair Trade coffee, for which producers are paid a higher, fairer price. Fair Trade coffee farmers in Colombia use the extra money to improve their farms, and to invest in better health and education services for their communities.

Unlike its neighbours, Brazil no longer relies on selling primary products. Instead, it has expanded its manufacturing industries. Since the 1950s, Brazilians have opened their own factories to take advantage of new markets in Europe, USA and neighbouring Argentina. Today, a quarter of Brazilians work in manufacturing, and many multinational companies have chosen to locate factories there. Brazil is now one of the world's biggest producers of steel, cars and petrochemicals. It is also a big exporter of TV programmes – to Europe, Africa and China. With a mixed economy, Brazil is better able to withstand changes in the international market. As a result, it makes more money than any other South American country, and had the thirteenth-largest economy in the world in 2003.

Bolivia is the continent's poorest country. Two-thirds of its population live in poverty and the country has the highest infant mortality rate in South America. Without direct access to the sea, Bolivians have to pay more to export and import goods. This increases the cost of Bolivian goods and makes them less attractive to buyers.

FACT FILE

Coffee is a major South American export. Brazil is the world's biggest coffee producer, and Colombia is the third-biggest.

Workers at a Chrysler plant in Brazil slowly lower the cab of a Dodge pickup truck.

President Lula da Silva talks to shantytown residents in Recife, northern Brazil, during the launch of an anti-hunger campaign in January 2003.

FACT FILE

Around 80 per cent of Brazil's farmland is owned by about 4 per cent of the population and 40 per cent of Brazilians live on less than 1 US dollar a day.

UNEQUAL BENEFITS

For all its newfound wealth, Brazil's riches are not evenly spread. Half its factories are in the south-east of the country. And much of Brazil's farmland is owned by a handful of wealthy families, leaving millions without any land at all. In 2002, Lula da Silva was elected as Brazil's president and brought new hope to Brazil's poor. Lula was born in the north-east, Brazil's poorest region. As a former shoe-shine boy and metal worker, Lula knows what it is like to be poor. He has promised to make the fight against hunger and poverty the top priority during his presidency.

DANGEROUSLY IN DEBT

Argentina's economic problems have been growing. Some people blame the government for wasting money and giving pay-offs to friends and allies. Others blame problems linked to debt. In the 1980s, Argentina took up offers of loans from overseas banks to pay for new developments. Interest rates were low in the 1980s. But when they later rose sharply, Argentina struggled to pay even the interest on the loans – let alone the debt itself.

To improve the situation, foreign banks and governments encouraged Argentina to remove trade barriers such as taxes on imported goods. With this 'free market',

Argentina was considered more likely to attract foreign investors. But the disadvantage was that Argentinian farmers and businesspeople no longer had any protection against foreign competition.

Unlike Brazil, which has an even bigger debt, the Argentinian economy could not grow fast enough to repay the money. In 2002, Argentina reached a crisis point. The total debt rose to US$155 billion, and the country was refused any more loans from overseas. Chaos followed. Argentina changed its president five times in 18 months. Unemployment skyrocketed, health and education services were cut, and a quarter of the country's children suffered from malnutrition. Meanwhile, Argentinian currency (the peso) fell by 70 per cent against the US dollar, and millions of Argentinians watched their hard-earned savings crash in value. For many, this was the last straw, and riots broke out across the capital, Buenos Aires. Now, although debt remains a burden, a sense of calm has returned, as ordinary Argentinians try to get on with their lives.

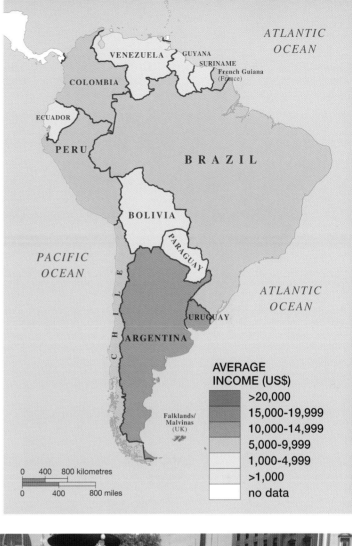

AVERAGE INCOME (US$)
- >20,000
- 15,000-19,999
- 10,000-14,999
- 5,000-9,999
- 1,000-4,999
- >1,000
- no data

0   400   800 kilometres

0   400   800 miles

Police carry away a demonstrator on the streets of Buenos Aires in December 2002.

47

7. SOUTH AMERICA IN THE WORLD

SOUTH AMERICA IS THE BIRTHPLACE OF SOME FOODS THAT PEOPLE IN THE REST of the world now take for granted. For instance, potatoes originally come from the Andes and have been farmed here since the time of the Incas in the early 1500s. Potatoes can grow on the steepest mountain slopes and in the thinnest of soils. The Aymara people cultivate as many as 400 different varieties of potato in the Andes.

A girl picking coca leaves near Quillabamba in Peru. Picking coca leaves is hard, poorly paid work.

For thousands of years, another crop called coca has been grown on the mountain slopes of the Andes. Millions of South Americans still buy coca leaves. They chew it or make coca tea as a remedy for the effects of high altitude, or even to ease the pain of childbirth. But coca is also the raw material for cocaine.

DRUGS AND VIOLENCE

The illegal production of cocaine turned a local culture into a multi-million dollar industry, especially in Colombia. Gangsters from Colombian cities, like Medellín, formed groups known as cartels to control the production of cocaine from coca leaves, and its illegal sale to drug users elsewhere. With their vast profits, drug cartels became very powerful. They used violence against competitors, and bribed police, politicians and customs officers to protect their business deals. Although the Colombian authorities had some success in arresting some of the cartel ringleaders, the drug trade remains strong. Today, rebel groups in Colombia control the cocaine trade, and drug trafficking has expanded into neighbouring Brazil and Ecuador.

FIGHTING THE DRUG WAR

The US government has been so alarmed by the flow of cocaine into the United States that it has given millions of dollars in aid to Colombia to fight the 'drug war'. As part of 'Plan Colombia', the United States is training and arming Colombian soldiers to fight cocaine dealers and smugglers. To destroy the coca crop, the soldiers spray it with chemicals or burn it, along with the buildings where the coca is processed to make cocaine. Yet, although cocaine abuse is a growing problem in South America, many people believe that the real problem lies with drug users in other countries. They argue that, so long as there is a demand, the drug trade will continue.

An armed soldier hangs out of a helicopter, looking for illegal coca fields in Colombia.

Encouraging coca farmers to grow other crops may be another way of destroying the cocaine trade. But many South American farmers cannot make enough money from other crops. They find it difficult to compete with farmers elsewhere who receive government subsidies (financial help) to grow crops more cheaply. In Europe and the United States, farmers not only receive subsidies, they are also protected by taxes on imported goods. However, farmers in the Andes have no such protection.

FACT FILE

The United States accounts for 75 per cent of the money made in North, South and Central America, and the US economy is 1,370 times bigger than Bolivia's.

Tourism is becoming an important industry in several South American countries. Growing numbers of South Americans are becoming tourists too.

A New Voice for the Poor World

To improve conditions in the region, Brazil, Argentina, Uruguay, Paraguay and Peru joined forces to form Mercosur, a common market where businesses can trade freely without paying extra taxes. The United States wants to create a free trade zone across most of the Americas, but critics argue that, without any protection, South American businesses could never compete with the USA. Instead, Argentina and Brazil are looking at ways to make Mercosur bigger and more powerful.

South American countries, with their neighbours in North and Central America and the Caribbean, are also members of the Organization of American States (OAS), which has its headquarters in Washington DC. The 35 member countries of the OAS are working together to promote peace and security, and to tackle international problems like terrorism and the illegal drug trade.

As the world's thirteenth-richest country, Brazil has a loud voice on the world stage. Every other year, Brazil holds a massive gathering of people called the 'World Social Forum' to share ideas on how to make the world a fairer place. Brazil also works closely with India and South Africa. These big developing countries are pushing for better trading conditions for poorer and less powerful nations.

The World Social Forum opens in Porto Alegre, Brazil.

••••••▶ IN FOCUS: Che Guevara

An Argentinian doctor called Ernesto 'Che' Guevara has become a worldwide symbol of idealism and rebellion. As a young man in the 1950s, Che travelled across the continent on his motorbike, and helped rebel movements in Mexico, Guatemala, Bolivia and Cuba. Che first met Fidel Castro, Cuba's President, in Mexico. When Castro seized power in the Cuban revolution of 1959, Che became Castro's chief lieutenant. As president of Cuba's national bank, Che was keen to cut ties to the United States because he believed the US opposed his vision of justice for the poor. With the help of the CIA, Bolivian troops captured and killed Che in the Andes in 1967.

A banner shows a likeness of Che Guevara during a rally in La Paz, Bolivia, held to mark International Labour Day in May 2004.

51

An Ariane rocket blasts off from the European Space Agency launch site at Kourou in French Guiana, in 2003.

OIL PRODUCERS

As the world's seventh-biggest oil producer, Venezuela can flex its muscles internationally as a member of the Organization of Petroleum Exporting Countries (OPEC). Together, OPEC members can influence the amount of oil that is pumped into the world marketplace. This way, they aim to keep oil prices stable and guarantee themselves a steady income. But, as more countries produce their own oil, and alternative energy sources (like tidal energy) become available, OPEC is losing some of its influence.

SOCCER STARS

The rest of the world has benefited from South America's rich culture as well. Spectators around the world

FACT FILE

French Guiana still has strong European links. For example, the European Space Agency launches rockets from French Guiana.

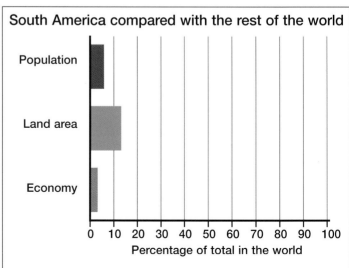

South America compared with the rest of the world

Population

Land area

Economy

0 10 20 30 40 50 60 70 80 90 100
Percentage of total in the world

Source: United Nations; World Bank; Britannica Book of the Year 2004

marvel at the skill of South American soccer players. A number of the continent's best players have moved to Europe to earn enormous salaries at top clubs there. Brazil has won the World Cup four times – more often than any other country.

TANGO

Music from South America can be heard all over the world. Tango was created in the slums of Buenos Aires. The first tango dancers were soldiers discharged from the army, or immigrants from Italy and Spain, who had arrived in the city's port to begin a new life. Lonely and homesick, these young men danced in pairs. With its fast, sensual rhythms, many people were shocked by tango, but, by the 1920s, it was all the rage in Paris and other European cities. Today, tango is having a revival back in its homeland. Young Argentinians are learning the complicated steps from their older relatives.

Tango dancers in Buenos Aires.

●●●●▶ IN FOCUS:
Diego Maradona

Diego Maradona was one of the greatest soccer players of all time. Born in a slum in Buenos Aires, he began his career with the Boca Juniors, one of the top clubs in Argentina. After playing for his country in the 1982 World Cup, Maradona moved to Europe, helping both Barcelona and Naples win a string of trophies. In 1986, he captained the Argentina team that went on to win the World Cup. During this championship, Maradona became a soccer legend after he scored an extraordinary goal against England. For many, this was the best goal in the history of the game.

8. SOUTH AMERICAN WILDLIFE

OVER ONE-THIRD OF THE WORLD'S 10,000 BIRD SPECIES LIVE IN SOUTH America. One of the most striking is the keel-billed toucan. The toucan's amazing beak is actually hollow and very light, but it is perfect for cracking open seeds for food. High in the treetops, toucans use their colourful beaks as flags, throwing their heads from side to side. Their distinctive call can be heard for miles. Meanwhile, millions of insects are busy on the forest floor. Leafcutter ants gather and chew leaves into a pulp, making a bed of fertilizer on which a special fungus grows. The ants then eat the fungus as food.

MAKING THE FOREST LAST

People in central Guyana are trying to use their tropical rainforest without destroying the forest itself. Run by local people, the Iwokrama Project covers almost 371,000 hectares (1,000,000 acres). Half the area is left undisturbed. The other half has become a centre for researchers, working with the Amerindians who live in the forest. Scientists can study the forest canopy from a new 20 m (65 foot) high walkway that has been built between the trees. A growing number of adventurous tourists are visiting Iwokrama too. Tourism brings in about US$120,000 a year. A lot of this money is used to help local villages and to train people as guides.

Toucans don't just eat fruits and berries. Sometimes they feed on small reptiles, or the eggs or young of other birds.

FACT FILE

The Amazon basin contains about a tenth of all the known plant, animal and insect species on Earth.

Piranhas are flesh-eating fish with razor-sharp teeth that live in the Amazon and its tributaries. But piranhas are not as dangerous as they are made out to be – they only attack if they smell blood. Another flesh-eater crouching on the riverbank is the caiman, a member of the alligator family. The Amazon river is also home to the pirarucu, the world's largest freshwater fish. Even though it grows up to 4 m (13 feet) long and weighs as much as 200 kg (440 lb), the pirarucu can still leap out of the water to grab young birds!

There are more than 10 million caiman alligators in the Brazilian Pantanal, one of the world's largest wetlands.

ABOVE THE CLOUDS

Soaring majestically above the Andes, with a wingspan of 3 m (9 feet), the condor is the world's largest flying bird. It can glide for up to an hour on mountain air currents. Condors are a kind of vulture, feeding off the remains of dead animals. They use their incredible eyesight to spot food from high in the sky.

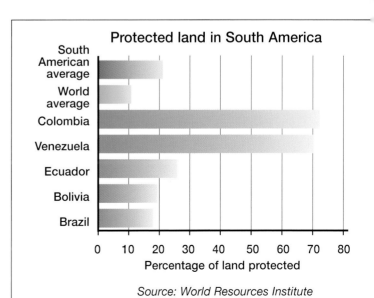

Protected land in South America

	Percentage of land protected
South American average	~21
World average	~11
Colombia	~72
Venezuela	~70
Ecuador	~26
Bolivia	~19
Brazil	~19

Source: World Resources Institute

Galibi, Suriname, is the largest breeding ground in the world for the endangered giant leatherback turtle. They can grow up to 2 metres (6 feet) long and can live to a grand old age of 50. In 1995, there were about 1,800 leatherback turtles and over 6,000 green turtles nesting at Galibi.

GUARDING TURTLES

Along the coast of Suriname, turtles come out of the sea at night and clamber up the remote stretch of sandy beach at Galibi. Here, they dig holes and lay their eggs in nests under the sand. But some species, like the green turtle and the leatherback, are very rare. They are under threat from people stealing their eggs, and from drowning after they get caught in fishing nets. Amerindians and conservationists are working together to protect the turtles in the Galibi nature reserve. To keep a check on their numbers, each turtle is measured and tagged when it comes ashore. No fishing is allowed for 15 km (9 miles) off the Galibi coast, and Amerindians from the local villages work as reserve wardens to keep a look-out for turtle egg thieves. The Amerindians also make money from tourists who come to stay in their villages to catch a glimpse of these magnificent creatures.

SOUTH AMERICAN PENGUINS

Alongside elephant seals, sea lions and millions of other birds, the sheer cliffs and barren plains of Peninsula Valdés, southern Argentina, are the summer home for over a million Magellanic penguins. The knee-high male penguins come ashore in early September to prepare a nest in a burrow underground before their partners arrive a few weeks later. After breeding, both parents take it in turn to feed their chicks until the young are ready to look after themselves. By February, the penguins return to the sea where they remain until the breeding season begins again.

Magellanic penguins are excellent swimmers. Using their wings as paddles, they can speed through the water at up to 24 km (15 miles) an hour.

●●●●●● ▶ IN FOCUS: 'Camel cousins'

The Andes are home to four relatives of the camel – llama, alpaca, vicuña and guanaco. Farmers on the *altiplano* domesticated llama and alpaca around 4000 BC, weaving, knitting and sewing their wool into garments. Today, alpaca wool even ends up in the fashion houses of Europe and the USA. Llamas make excellent pack animals. Sure-footed on mountain slopes, llamas can carry up to 60 kg (132 lb). Packs of wild vicuña graze on the marshlands of the *altiplano*. People say that vicuña wool is the softest thing in the world. Guanacos are their larger, southern relatives, with thicker coats to survive the freezing winters in Patagonia.

Guanacos in the Torres del Paine National Park, Chile.

9. THE FUTURE OF SOUTH AMERICA

As more people all over the world move to cities, we need to find new, less environmentally harmful ways of living together in large numbers. Curitiba, in Brazil, may be a model for the future. Here, local people are involved in future plans so that new developments meet their needs. With 17 parks and 150 km (90 miles) of bicycle lanes, many residents of Curitiba think they live in the best city in the world. Nearly two thousand buses carry passengers on special bus lanes that criss-cross the city.

Curitiba's transport network prioritizes public transport over private car drivers. The network also links together different kinds of public transport, enabling more Curitiba residents to travel easily and cheaply across the city.

Although it has ten times as many people as it had 50 years ago, Curitiba offers residents, including the city's street children, a better quality of life. Offices and shops pay street children to do odd jobs in order to give them a means of supporting themselves.

YOUNG PEACEMAKERS

Colombians are hoping for a more peaceful future. Armed conflict between guerrilla groups and the Colombian army has been dragging on for nearly forty years. The guerrillas want the government to give Colombia's poor a better deal, including a fairer share of the country's land. But some see the guerrillas as

A young girl working with UNICEF (the United Nations Children's Fund) and the Children's Peace Movement talks to a soldier about their campaign for peace, in Medellín, Colombia.

terrorists who use violence and kidnapping to scare people. Today, younger people are speaking out against the war, and older generations are starting to listen. The Children's Movement for Peace is campaigning for the right to a peaceful future. Roughly a third of the country's young people are now involved in the campaign.

DEVELOPMENT THAT LASTS

Important and difficult choices lie ahead for people who live in the Amazon basin. The Amazon rainforest is an immense resource that must be carefully used, and the livelihood of millions depends on it. Brazil plans to create more farms, roads, dams and natural gas pipelines through the region, but these developments could destroy a quarter of Brazil's tropical rainforest. Yet there are ways to make money from the forest without destroying it. Small projects that harvest forest products like rubber and nuts already help people in ways that last. Also, medicines have been developed from Amazonian plants, like penicillin (developed from a rainforest fungus) and quinine, a treatment for malaria. These discoveries have already helped people worldwide. So long as the rainforest is kept intact, some scientists hope that a cure for HIV/AIDS may one day be found in a rainforest plant.

STATISTICAL COMPENDIUM

Nation	Area (sq km)	Population (2003)	Urbanization (% population) 2003	Life expectancy at birth 2002 (in years)	GDP per capita (US$) 2002	Percentage of population under 15 years 2003	Percentage of population over 65 years 2003
Argentina	2,780,092	38,428,000	90.1	74.1	10,880	27	10
Bolivia	1,098,581	8,808,000	63.4	63.7	2,460	38	4
Brazil	8,547,404	178,470,000	83.1	68.0	7,770	27	5
Chile	756,626	15,805,000	87.0	76.0	9,820	27	7
Colombia	1,141,568	44,222,000	76.5	72.1	6,370	31	5
Ecuador	272,045	13,003,000	61.8	70.7	3,580	33	5
French Guiana (France)	86,504	178,000	75.4	N/a	N/a	N/a	N/a
Guyana	215,083	765,000	37.6	63.2	4,260	30	5
Paraguay	406,752	5,878,000	57.2	70.7	4,610	39	4
Peru	1,285,216	27,167,000	73.9	69.7	5,010	32	5
Suriname	163,820	436,000	76.1	71.0	6,590	29	5
Uruguay	176,215	3,415,000	92.6	75.2	7,830	24	13
Venezuela	912,050	25,699,000	87.7	73.6	5,830	32	5

Sources: UN Agencies, World Bank and Britannica

GLOSSARY

Altitude The height of the land above sea level, sometimes known as elevation.

Cartel A group of people, companies or countries that work together to control the supply and price of a product, e.g. drugs.

Coca A plant that grows in bushes, and is the raw material for producing cocaine.

Co-operative A company or organization that is jointly owned and run by the people who work there or share in its benefits.

Coral reef Corals are actually animals called polyps. Thousands join together to make up one reef.

Coup When a group of people suddenly get together to try to overthrow those in power.

Cross-breeding Breeding an animal or plant with another animal or plant.

Crust The outer layer of the Earth.

Dictatorship A form of government in which the ruler (or dictator) has complete power.

Domesticated (Usually of a plant or animal) adapted to suit the needs of people.

Drug cartel A group of people who work together to control trade in illegal drugs.

Epiphyte A plant that grows on soil particles trapped in the branches of another plant.

Equator The imaginary line around the centre of the Earth that divides the northern hemisphere and the southern hemisphere.

Fair Trade A system under which producers are paid a fair price for their produce.

Glacier A huge mass of ice slowly flowing over the land, formed from compressed snow.

Global warming The gradual warming of the Earth's atmosphere as a result of carbon dioxide emissions and other greenhouse gases trapping heat.

Gourd A hollowed-out bowl made of wood, pumpkin or even silver.

Guerrilla A member of an independent armed group that fights against the rulers of a territory to force a change in the balance of power.

Hydro-electric power (HEP) A type of energy generated by fast-flowing water flowing through turbines.

Independence When a country wins the right to control its own affairs.

Infant mortality The number of babies, out of every 1,000 born, who die before the age of one.

Infertility Inability to have children.

Irrigation The artificial watering of land to help crops grow. Normally practised in areas of low or unreliable rainfall.

Landlocked Without a coast but surrounded by land.

Latitude Distance north or south of the equator. The equator is 0 degrees latitude.

Lent The 40 days before the religious holiday of Easter when Christians fast, pray and give money to the poor.

Lithium A soft, silver-white substance that is the lightest known metal.

Malaria A tropical disease transmitted to people by mosquito bites. It causes severe flu-like symptoms and, if not treated, can lead to death in some cases.

Malnutrition Deficiency in the nutrients that are essential for the development of the body and its maintenance in adulthood.

Multinational company A company that owns and operates manufacturing or service businesses in several countries. A company that operates in more than one country is described as transnational.

Nitrate A chemical fertilizer.

Plantation A type of farm found in tropical areas. A plantation usually covers a large area and grows one or two types of crop.

Plate A large section of the Earth's crust.

Plateau A flat, raised area of land.

Richter scale A scale measuring the amount of energy released by an earthquake.

Smelting Separating metal from a rock by melting it in extreme heat in a furnace.

Subsidy Money provided by the government to keep the price of a product or service low, or to help pay the producers of a product or service.

Trade winds Tropical winds that blow towards the equator from the north-east (northern hemisphere) and the south-east (southern hemisphere).

Tributary A river or stream that flows into another, normally larger, one.

Tsunami A very large ocean wave caused by an earthquake or volcanic eruption beneath the sea.

Urban sprawl The gradual spread of an urban centre outwards.

FURTHER INFORMATION

BOOKS TO READ:

A River Journey: The Amazon Simon Scoones (Hodder Wayland, 2003)

Andes to the Amazon: A guide to wild South America Michael Bright (BBC Consumer Publishing, 2000)

Are we there yet?: The Europeans meet the Americans (*Horrible Histories* series) Elizabeth Levy (Scholastic, 2002)

The Changing Face of Peru Don Harrison and Janet Ramirez (Hodder Wayland, 2003)

The Changing Face of Brazil Ed Parker (Hodder Wayland, 2004)

The Changing Face of Argentina Daisy and Les Fearns (Hodder Wayland, 2004)

An Illustrated Atlas of South America Keith Lye and Malcolm Porter (Cherry Tree Books, 1999)

USEFUL WEBSITES:

www.survival-international.org
Survival International is a worldwide organization supporting tribal peoples.

http://gosouthamerica.about.com/cs/travelplanning/l/blvirttour.htm
Take a virtual tour of South America.

http://kids.ran.org/kidscorner/index.html
Rainforest Action Network's website for young people.

www.globaleye.org.uk
An interactive website, with features on Brazil, Colombia, Peru, the Amazon, Guyana and the Iwokrama project.

www.geography.learnontheinternet.co.uk/topics/rainforest.html
Find out more about rainforests and how people are using them.

www.mrdowling.com/712southamerica.html
Interesting facts about the land and people of South America.

http://worldatlas.com/webimage/countrys/sa.htm
For maps and information about different South American countries.

www.gridclub.com/info/atlas/s_am_map.shtml
Use an interactive map of South America to find out about key features of the continent.

www.odci.gov/cia/publications/factbook/
Offers the CIA facts and figures on every country.